MAGIC OF THE WOODS

MAX ALBERT WYSS

MAGIC OF THE WOODS

A STUDIO BOOK · THE VIKING PRESS · NEW YORK

And for all this, nature is never spent;

There lives the dearest freshness deep down things

GERARD MANLEY HOPKINS
from "God's Grandeur"

MAGIC OF THE WOODS

Man is inclined to take nature for granted, to accept it without curiosity or question. We become aware of things and events only when they come close to us, when they affect us spiritually or physically and penetrate our consciousness as being out-of-the-ordinary, significant and moving experiences.

The earlier the individual comes into contact with experiences of this kind—such as a child's awe of his first thunderstorm, or a young man's response to the alluring promise of foreign shores—the deeper and more enduring will be his faculty for perceiving and experiencing nature.

Nature has been thrust so far out to the edge of modern life that most of the time man is obliged to live without it altogether. This is recognized as a deprivation only when the inborn feeling for nature has not entirely atrophied. But what is the Sunday migration of thousands of men, women, and children from the cities to the sea, lakes, or mountains other than a desperate attempt to return to nature? And even when this impulse to escape from the artificiality and constraint of everyday life is turned into a lucrative business, a vestige of benefit to the individual remains.

The urge to seek spiritual and physical benefit in the woods is by no means new: even in the unhurried decades of the nineteenth century, when dreary housing conditions and air pollution had not yet become ubiquitous, families would set out cheerily and decorously for a day in the country. Frequent expeditions to the woods and open fields were a recognized part of middle-class life, and lessons in observation were regarded less as instruction than as pleasant outings by nature-loving children. These excursions found their echo in orderly collections of pressed wildflowers and, when the experience penetrated deeper, in rapturous and sentimental outpourings in young ladies' diaries, where a yearning for sylvan solitude was mingled with other nameless longings.

Away, away, from men and towns,
To the wild woods and the downs—
To the silent wilderness
Where the soul need not repress
Its music, lest it should not find
An echo in another's mind,
While the touch of Nature's art
Harmonizes heart to heart.

Percy Bysshe Shelley
from "The Invitation"

We may smile at so much romanticism; but the fact remains that in those days familiarity with nature was considered as much of an attribute as good manners. Altered social circumstances and conditions have resulted in the dying out of many customs and traditions, but nevertheless an unsatisfied longing for nature has remained. Recognition of the need for a relationship to nature has taken the place of ecstatic romanticism, and enjoyment of nature has become a common sense recipe for moral and spiritual gain which, assisted by modern means of transportation, is becoming more easily and rapidly accessible all the time. Walks in the suburban woods, meadows, and manorial parks of the old days have been replaced by excursions to the last available nature reserves: unspoiled woods, green wildernesses.

But do they really still exist?

I believe so. Within an hour's train journey from most cities the woods still exist, even if they are little more than oases in the civilized landscape. Rivers bordered by thick lines of trees, wooded hilltops as yet unconquered by the machine, valleys melting into an expanse of woodland, and untouched forests on the sides of mountains which call a natural halt to the spread of civilization—the woods are not yet lost to us!

We can find the way back to them, and we can rely on them; we can sense and perceive their greatness, their strength, and their magic.

THE WOODS
HAVE THEIR HISTORY

Like most natural phenomena, woods and forests in all parts of the world are as inconstant in their dimensions and composition as rivers or lakes. Thus the origin, evolution, and possible disappearance of wooded areas must be viewed in the light of the general progress of terrestrial development and the continual and eternal stream of change in nature.

The glaciers which covered wide expanses of Europe and North America during the last Ice Age destroyed vast regions of woodland vegetation, and it was in only a few sheltered areas that some mountain pines, willows, and birches managed to survive; in the remaining glacier-free districts it was either the tundra mosses and lichens or the arctic-alpine dwarf birches and willows which endured. At the end of the Ice Age Europe and Canada were almost entirely devoid of wooded regions, and it was only gradually that the ousted tree species returned to the fringe areas. The pine and spruce, the fir and the beech returned gradually from other areas—tenacious and indestructible, unyielding in their power of growth, they were bearers and harbingers of new life.

The woods flourished on the earth once more, and in them prospered animals, birds, flowers, and fruit. But the milder period around 1300 B.C.—which was probably warmer than the present—was followed by another deterioration in climate. The hardy, cold-resistant pines and spruces spread over the meadowland of Central Europe, only to be met by fire and axes; for medieval man's dependence on acorns and beech mast for pig food compelled him to protect the deciduous trees at the expense of the conifers. It is hardly possible to estimate the extent of this unscrupulous forestry during the course of the following three centuries, but it is certain that the composition of woods in populated areas could no longer be considered natural as early as the middle of the eighteenth century. When we consider that

CAPTIONS TO THE PICTURES:

Page 9   Red deer on the alert
Pages 10/11 The great silence
Page 12   Beech woods in the rain

8

THE RED BRANCH

Sky after sky of windless blue;
warm days, but with a secret chill.
The forest wall is green except
for one red branch on the hill.

Quiet the leaves, as on a board
dead butterflies are pinned,
except for one red branch that stirs
in premonition of a wind.

Soon the September gale, too soon
the bare branch, the leaves blown.
Now, in the mid-September truce,
one leaf drifts down.

Malcolm Cowley

replanting of the cleared and empty areas was not contemplated except occasionally on a purely local basis, the use of the word "plunder" does not seem exaggerated.

It would probably be possible to produce evidence to show that most of the woods in Central Europe at the end of the eighteenth century were literally destitute—and the condition of the wild animals was no better. The woods were much less rich in game 150 years ago than they are today, and when we read of the sporting deeds of the absolute monarchs and their courts, we must not forget that they usually took place in enclosed and protected reserves which nurtured specially bred red deer. In North America, the seemingly limitless forests and endless abundance of wildlife which greeted the early settlers were so ruthlessly exploited that many species soon became extinct or survive today only in guarded areas.

The "century of economic and industrial prosperity" helped itself to timber without restraint. The ever-increasing numbers of houses necessary for the growing population had to be heated, almost every trade used wood as raw material, boat and railway-track builders consumed whole forests of oak, and the young iron industry devoured immeasurable quantities of firewood. The increase in cattle farming cleared away vast areas of woodland, and the repeated plowing of marginal land which might better have been left in its natural state resulted in a process of erosion which turned woods and meadows into near-deserts.

The woods suffered from drought, from fire, from insect plagues—but most of all they suffered from the greed and folly of man, a folly rooted in human nature itself. For in his constant concern for his immediate needs and continual struggle for more and more of all that life has to offer, man is seldom capable of thinking in terms of generations. Instead of planting oaks for the benefit of his grandchildren and great-grandchildren, he plants fast-growing firs for use in his own lifetime.

Compared to nature, man is short-lived not only in years but in character and deeds as well. And shortsighted too. . . .

But the forest cannot die.

It is strong, powerful, and enduring, possessed of the vitality and vigor that nature bestows upon her creatures, which are all rooted in and interwoven with the soil, indestructible and abiding.

For many years now it has been my practice to look out for unusual trees wherever I travel, much in the way that one tends to keep an eye open for interesting personalities and, whenever possible, tries to establish contact with them. I was always conscious that the ancient, inborn desire for the discovery of the unknown must lie behind this urge, but in this case the result was that I was unable to see the wood for the trees. I failed to experience the woods as a natural, integrated whole, as part of creation and a source of a nameless joy and satisfaction.

A really close relationship to the woods may be possible only if you have missed them deeply at some time or other. Thus, in a way, it should be a cause for gratitude to have once lived in regions where the woods are as rare as cool spring water, snow, or newly mown grass. If you have been in Africa you may conjure up a memory of the forest— a different forest, uncanny, frighteningly still, and filled with the odors of mold and carrion . . . a tedious, apathetic evergreen landscape found only in the jungle, in which silent butterflies devoid of radiance and color reel giddily like blind creatures between atrophied tree trunks and snakelike creepers. Or you may recall the giant mountain forests which surround Kilimanjaro, remember being entangled in man-high ferns, being feverish and bathed in cold sweat, in your ears the fancied sounds of elephants whose freshly steaming droppings you encountered on the narrow path as you stumbled on ahead of the African bearers, hour after hour in the damp green confusion, for a day, for two days, around you an unending greenness even where there should be sky. . . . Or perhaps you remember driving through a forest of dead trees: like bleached bones, the wretched remains of trees destroyed by termites sticking up all around you from the ash-gray ground; ghostly and completely silent, skeleton after skeleton slipping by in ever-changing perspective as you continued on your harrowing journey with labored breath, your sticky hands clenched on the steering wheel as if on the barrel of a gun. . . . Is it surprising that you longed for the woods of home, for the resin-scented pine forests, for the velvet of the woodland carpet and the pale green of the beech leaves in spring?

But perhaps it is just this deeply buried memory of the wilderness which is the origin of a new relationship to the woods and which kindles the urge to seek in them a lost paradise, to look for a world in

Some time now past in the Autumnal Tide,
When Phoebus wanted but one hour to bed,
The trees all richly clad, yet void of pride,
Were gilded o'er by his rich golden head.
Their leaves and fruits seemed painted, but was true
Of green, of red, of yellow, mixed hue,
Rapt were my senses at this delectable view.

Anne Bradstreet
from "Contemplations"

which animals live in freedom and plants follow undisturbed their own rules of growth, a world in which man can only be a guest—a silent observer, a wanderer, or a naturalist according to his temperament and understanding, but in all cases a seeker for refuge in an undefinable and enigmatic world of surety.

But this aura of surety and peace can change as suddenly as the weather: a heavy cloud settles unexpectedly over the woods and the gentle twilight is transformed into a threatening darkness; the wood freezes into uncanny stillness before the approaching storm. In late autumn, mists haunt the stream valleys, become entangled in the boughs and bushes, and muffle the final whisper of the last remaining leaves. In the depths of winter the erring skier may fall prey to a fear of cold amounting almost to panic as he searches for the path through the high, frozen woods in which white, empty-eyed solitude lingers between the gray tree trunks, and there is no sound but the whining of the wind in the ice-bound pine needles. . . .

But always, year after year, the spring returns. The life force awakes once more; the leaves and flowers sprout and the fruit ripens. Another woodland year awaits us, and we go forth to greet and welcome it as a friend!

ABUNDANCE OF LIFE

Much of the benefit I have gained from the woods over many years of exploration and observation I owe to a man who himself cherished a very special relationship to the woods. He operated a sawmill in the foothills of the mountains and was also entrusted by the community with a number of jobs in the near-by alpine forest where the cool mountain streams started on their course into the valley below. In addition, he was a hunter. He knew—as the local people used to say—the places! So did his children, whom I often accompanied on mushroom- and berry-picking expeditions. He knew the haunts of the heathcock, the times when the deer came out of the wood to graze in the open, and where the stoat hunted at dusk. He knew which trees were frequented by woodpeckers, the best juniper bushes, and all the foxes in his province. He was a simple and contented man who had his own brand of humor, and the woods and their inhabitants meant more to him than books and learning. I think he loved the woods in the same way that he loved his wife, his children, his rifle, the scent of resin from freshly sawn pines, and the sharp aroma of autumn when he went hunting. In the hunting season this usually quiet and reflective man would be overtaken by a restlessness which drove him from his home and work. It was the woods which called him, the woods to which he owed his living and his freedom.

I believe it was the woods and his life with them which made him what he was.

I am especially grateful to him for the way he taught me to see. His method of initiation was not to draw my attention in words to animals and plants which I might otherwise have missed in the dimness of the woods. He would simply pause at the sight of the falling scale of a fir cone or the sound of a soft, hollow hammering, and I too would look up and see something in the branches—a beady-eyed squirrel, or a red-crested woodpecker. Before he stepped into a clearing, he would always

All Nature seems at work.
Slugs leave their lair—
The bees are stirring—
birds are on the wing—
And Winter slumbering in the
open air,
Wears on his smiling face a dream
of Spring!

Samuel Taylor Coleridge
from "Work without Hope"

stand motionless behind a tree for a while and scour the trees and bushes with his binoculars; and so it came about that I saw a fleeting pine marten for the first time, and learned to recognize the buzzard in the treetops before it flew away. He taught me to approach the woodland animals against the wind and to follow the stream uphill. And so, in the wild, hidden, and almost inaccessible gully of a stream I discovered for the first time the secret, unknown life of the woods.

I was a long way away from the more frequented areas of the wood that bore the traces of the ax and old campfires when I caught a glimpse of light through the trees and a warm, damp gust of wind wafted a heavy, musty scent toward me. I pushed my way through the bushes, stumbling over slippery stones, and finally arrived at the edge of a glade. There before me was a green, light-sprinkled wilderness. Then I saw the horsetails—knee-high, crowded densely together, prolific as jungle vegetation. They grew out of the black peaty soil, penetrated the leafy undergrowth and spread along the brownish channels of stagnant water up onto the drier banks, thinned out gradually into isolated specimens growing around rotten tree stumps on which sun-warmed fern fronds softly rose and fell. And there, where the gully of the stream lost itself in the wood once more, the pink and white umbels of the giant hogweed floated in the woodland twilight like swaying islands in a green confusion, heavy with a strange scent and a multitude of insects.

Honey-colored bumblebees landed clumsily on the sea of blossom; green-gold and iridescent flies sunned themselves beside busy, crawling ladybirds; beetles felt their way out of the froth of blossom with their sensitive, vestless antennae; dragonflies glided gleaming to and fro; and now and then a butterfly for which I had no name settled on the blossom in a haze of color.

Also unspecified at the time were the small gray spiders, the shield-bearing bugs, the long-legged mosquitoes, the insects with long proboscises, and the delicately veined snails; and how confusing and incomprehensible was their bustling activity. Much as I would have liked to take this man-high, white-decked, honey-yielding table home with me, I could not bring myself to disturb the world I had just discovered.

Not all encounters in the woods are as peaceful and contemplative as this. But although I was once obliged to beat a hasty retreat under the hostile stare of a fallow buck who clearly felt my presence to be undesirable, I have never had to run from a wild boar, as some of my acquaintances have.

As early as World War I, whole sounders of boar fled from the Black Forest of Germany across the bridges over the Rhine into neutral Switzerland, usually by night and with a supreme disregard for customs' formalities. There was even a rumor that a group of wild boar had been seen crashing through a splintering customs' barrier—the witnesses to this event observed the occurrence from an elevated position providently surrounded by barbed wire. Whether or not this report is true, it is certain that many a farmer whose land lay on the borders of the dense woods along the Rhine exchanged his hoes and shovels for a rifle when he left the village, and more than once a road worker or a homeward-bound factory hand was obliged to spend two or more uncomfortable hours on a woodpile in the wintry woods before the boars retreated and enabled him to reclaim his bicycle and pedal to safety—if the wheels still had all their spokes intact! Certainly many a teacher in an isolated village often waited in vain for his pupils who had been detoured on their way to school by boar obstructing their path. Today's visitor to the woods is not likely to suffer an experience of this kind—unless, of course, he should happen to find himself in one of Germany's big-game reserves and his path should cross that of a sounder of wild boar on their way to the slough. If so, he would be well advised not to pick up the prettily striped young piglets and stroke them behind the ears; their penetrating squeals are sure to summon the angry sow and even angrier boar, and since no fairy-tale house of refuge will appear close at hand, the only salvation will probably lie in the branches of the nearest tree.

It would be interesting to ask a reliable hunter about the outcome of his encounters with wild boar. There is not much evidence available, for it seems that wild boar are at the bottom of the list of European hunters—unless they happen to be guests of highly official state hunts and have the privilege of admiring the "bag" in the company of foreign ministers, secretaries of state, or even crowned heads.

Perhaps there are people whose estimation of a wood bears a direct relation to its content of game. This attitude does not necessarily open them to criticism, especially when they contribute to the preservation and well-being of the animals. In any case, we would be guilty of a

Now let my bed be hard,
  Nor care take I;
I'll make my joy like this
  Small Butterfly,
Whose happy heart has power
To make a stone a flower.

W. H. Davies
from "The Example"

regrettable shortsightedness and lack of understanding to refuse to accept the ancient hunting instinct in man. The word "criminal" in its true sense can be applied only to those who thoughtlessly and heartlessly destroy young wildlife.

Probably we can benefit spiritually and materially from nature's abundance of life only if we are prepared to take the trouble to participate in it. We live in a civilization in which nature—in the sense of flora and fauna which have grown and developed according to their natural patterns—plays a limited role in everyday life. Every woodsman knows that he must fight for "his" wood, and as trustee of an economically important and idealistically significant natural inheritance he is, to a great extent, dependent on the cooperation and good will of nature lovers. Only with our collaboration is it possible to preserve the emotionally and materially valuable woodland which can enrich our lives so immeasurably and give us an insight into a natural and meaningful world.

The abundance I mention is not abundance in the sense of quantity and magnitude: it is abundance of life itself, the richness of creation in all its forms. Each individual can perceive it in his own way—emotionally or scientifically—according to his disposition. To one man the hovering of a dragonfly is an inexplicable miracle, to another it is a problem of muscle and motion; the blue of a cornflower may be a beautiful but self-evident phenomenon for me, whereas you may ask what nature's purpose is in creating this intensity of blue; the naïve man is overcome by wonder at the ceaseless activity of an anthill, and his more analytical brother will attempt to solve the riddle of the organization and purpose of insect communities.

From this great wonder a new feeling for nature evolves—an awe of all creation and a boundless respect for the miraculous order in the abundance of life.

ROOTS IN DARKNESS, CROWNS IN LIGHT

Intelligent children can drive adults almost to distraction with their incessant questions. But in fact there is much to be said for their interminable "Why?" We, who after all expect from children so much zest for knowledge, are burdened by the guilt of our own ignorance. Adults ought to know about things! They ought to know why the trees are green, whether they breathe like humans, and sleep and dream and . . . and . . . and. . . .

So, stimulated by the child's lust for knowledge, you turn once more to your old exercise books and long-forgotten textbooks, only to find that there is nothing in them about why trees are green. True, the function of chlorophyll is explained, and you learn that the green of plants is determined by pigments of which two are green and two are orange-yellow, and that they absorb red and blue light. . . . But what can the word "absorb" mean to a child? So you try to explain more simply by saying that chlorophyll produces sugar from water and carbon with the help of the sun's warmth in a wonderful and mysterious way which is hard for a child to understand, and that the resulting starch is nourishing. "You know, like the starch in bread and corn."

The child accepts the bit about the starch and the bread but is unable to understand why you have changed the subject from leaves to bread when all that he wanted to know was why leaves are green. However, a hint that your efforts are not quite in vain is afforded by the question: "Where are the yellow pigments—are they what we see in autumn?"

"Quite right—well done," you say, and, delighted at so much childish intelligence, you add that in autumn the green pigments die first, the yellows and reds survive a little longer, and finally the leaves die altogether. "Do you understand?"

The child understands well enough because he has experienced this dying in the dry rustling of autumn leaves which "sound so sad" when he shuffles through them. "Do the trees die every year?"

Who looks through nature with an eye
That would the scheme of heaven descry,

Observes her constant, still the same,
In all her laws, through all her frame.

Philip Freneau
from "On the Uniformity and Perfection of Nature"

"They don't really die—it's more like sleep. Like a long, deep, peaceful sleep. And then in spring, as you know, the trees wake up again. . . ."

The fact that it is only the garment of the tree which becomes discolored and dies each year is comforting to adults as well as to children. It also makes it easier to explain to the child that trees are living organisms which take their moisture and nourishment from the soil and warmth from the sun in order to grow tall and strong—just like human beings. Of course, they cannot move away from rain, cold, or danger, but they do breathe, and at night they rest, although they do not sleep. . . .

"Why not?"

How inadequate is our vocabulary when it comes to passing on our little bit of knowledge of nature to a child! Do trees really not sleep because a stream of sap—like the blood of human beings—flows continually from their hidden roots to their topmost leaves?

What does it matter if a child believes that the resin which oozes from a wounded tree is blood? Did not Schiller, in his "William Tell," speak of trees bleeding when they were struck by the ax, thus alluding to the vulnerability of all living things? "The trees are all bewitched, and—whoe'er injures them—his hand . . . will grow out from the grave," he warns, thus stating with poetic impact that he who fells the trees which protect the valley from "the glaciers that send down avalanches, and thunder so at night" commits a crime.

My woodsman friend once told me that woodcutters inspect a tree carefully before they fell it, just as one might examine a man upon whose life one has designs. It may be superstitious to say that a tree knows how to revenge itself—but how many trees have killed their slayers as they fell?

The underground life of the tree begins where the gray roots creep snakelike into the soil. The tree seeks nourishment in the earth, absorbs water and mineral salts and conveys them through secret channels in the trunk up into the leafy, breathing boughs.

Inadequate as the word "structure" may sound, it is nevertheless applicable: a tree is a structure with foundations, pillars, arches, and roof—a constantly growing, self-rejuvenating structure, a miracle of living architecture and a symbol of life rising from the darkness of the soil into the light.

Who would deny that trees are beautiful? How can we ever see enough of their proud growth and strong personalities? Of the drooping shoulders of the spruce; the mossy dignity of the old sycamore; the motherly, protective beech; the bountiful lime; the green torches of the poplar; the grandeur of the oak; the rippling leaves of the birch; the mystery of the dark yew in the deep silence of the woods?

It is not surprising that some species of tree were sacred to early man. The lime, for example, was dedicated to a goddess of fertility and thus became the tree of lovers who dreamed their dreams beneath its shady boughs. The poet Hermann Hiltbrunner, who associated with trees almost as if they were human beings and made them his companions, wrote of them in these words: "In the pale moonlight, I can see the heart of the tree, a heart born of its thousands and thousands of leaves. I hear the night wind come and go in its branches; when it comes, it comes on the pinions of secret longing and when it goes, it goes like a lover. It passes by me as it leaves, and its breath has taken on a sweetness; it breathes the fragrance of the tree which it has visited. . . ."

Not everyone is blessed with the sensibility and sensitivity of a poet, and those who are often have no words to express their emotions. But what does this matter? Trees and woods exist. They affect us uniquely and gladden us like an unearned, unexpected present. No one who has known the young green of deciduous woods, the dignity of mighty, soaring pine forests, or the jubilation of birds in the rain-washed treetops can ever forget the experience. And unforgettable in the woodland year are the towering of red, glowing larches against the blue-black sky and the metallic radiance of pines beneath the falling light. And the wind, surging, soaring through the woods. . . .

The trees are like a sea;
Tossing,
Trembling,
Roaring,
Wallowing,
Darting their long green flickering fronds
    up at the sky,
Spotted with white blossom-spray.

The trees are roofs:
Hollow caverns of cool blue shadow,
Solemn arches
In the afternoons.
The whole vast horizon
In terrace beyond terrace,
Pinnacle above pinnacle,
Lifts to the sky
Serrated ranks of green on green.

JOHN GOULD FLETCHER
from "Green Symphony"

EYES OF AMBER

The last vestige of light between the trees had faded and the outlines of the leaves and branches were indistinct and blurred. The gray roots of the pines were undistinguishable from the mossy stones, and the woodland path was lost in the spider-webby dimness. It was so still that I fancied I heard sounds which did not exist. But—there it was again: a sigh, a soft moan. Something glided through the air; here—there—nowhere. And once again the soft, complaining call, far off yet close, a whimper which abruptly ceased.

I was sitting, hot and weary, beneath the trees when I suddenly had the feeling that I was being watched! A shudder ran down my spine, and I was tempted to stand up, shout, or reach for a stick. And then I saw it; sitting before the blackness of a hollow, gray, unmoving, and uncanny. A bird? Its stare was steadfast and penetrating, and its eyes were huge, round, and cold. And yellow—an evil yellow. The yellow of amber.

Then suddenly, soundlessly, it was gone. I could still feel the coldness of its staring eyes on me as I heard it once again, far off now, a dark, sad call. And I realized that its stare, like its call, was not really evil, only sad, questioning, and enigmatic.

When I told my woodsman friend of this encounter with the owl, he suggested that it was probably either a hawk owl or a long-eared owl. Certainly not a brown or tawny owl, for they were rare in the district and their eyes are almost black. He accepted without question my assertion that the bird had "sighed and wailed" like a sick child. He also told me that his wife feared the mournful cry of the screech owl, especially when someone in the district was ill; it seems that there are still people who believe the owl to be a bird of ill omen.

In the same year I also saw a great black woodpecker for the first time. If it had not been for my friend's children I would never have noticed it, for it sat so high up in an old spruce that at first sight I saw

only a jet-black bird hammering away at the bark of the tree as if obsessed. The harsh staccato of its beak rang through the tall woods as the bird ardently and unconcernedly pursued its carpentry work. I did not notice the scarlet marking on the back of its head until it leaned back in typical woodpecker fashion, evidently to review its work; it never spared us a glance.

I learned to follow the sounds made by birds, the soft rasping of claws and the rustling of the dry foliage. I also made the acquaintance of the tree creeper, which looks like a piece of pine bark come to life. And I observed with delight the way the wryneck repeatedly glances over its shoulder as if it were expecting someone any minute. I watched the merry, never-tiring antics of the tits with much enjoyment, and one day I was delighted to discover a hoopoe with its feathery crown and delicately banded wings, which it uses like fans, almost negligently. I learned that many birds live entirely in hiding, in the dense under-growth, in the topmost branches of the tallest trees, in fissures in rock, and in holes in the ground. The activity of the birds is never-ceasing: scratching, pecking, burrowing, searching with sharp beaks for beetles, caterpillars, worms, spiders, snails, wood ants, butterflies, bees, wasps, berries, and seeds; flitting through the foliage; tripping over the ground and stones; swinging on slender branches; running up tree trunks and down again headfirst; hanging on fir cones, scratching at the bark and propping themselves up on their tails like woodpeckers. Somewhere a hawk crouches in a thicket on the edge of a clearing and swoops suddenly and maliciously on a harmless mouse or thrush. Or a sparrow hawk skims over a hedge and scours the wood for prey and hurls itself upon a small bird or mouse.

For death too lurks in the woods—in sunshine, in the twilight, and at night. Wherever there is life and plenty there is also death and decay. Birds enjoy only a short life span of half a dozen to a dozen years—or perhaps we should say summers. Certainly time scales differ in nature among the species, and the time of year as determined by the sun is especially important to the birds. Birds live with the sun, and it is surely significant that the migration of many summer visitors coincides in some mysterious way with the summer solstice. Birds of passage arrange their migration—or so the experts tell us—according to the changing position of the sun, and the fact that night-flying birds take their bearings by the stars bears witness to their strongly visual nature.

To one who has been long in city
pent,
'Tis very sweet to look into the fair
And open face of heaven,—to
breathe a prayer
Full in the smile of the blue
firmament.

John Keats
from "To One Who Has Been
Long in City Pent"

Light is probably also the incentive for their song. The popular belief that the blackbird and wren greet the sun with their singing is in fact correct, even though they often begin long before sunrise. It seems that something mysterious emanates from light, penetrates the eye of the bird, and enters its "soul" as a stimulus which is released in song.

"Empty words!" you may say. "Theories, conjectures!"

You may be right, and perhaps I should not have used the word "soul." But if not soul, then at least spirit—a spirit possessed of a quality we could call sensibility. Perhaps it is going too far to say that birds have a feeling of responsibility for their young; but anyone who has watched the tireless patience and devotion with which a pair of birds nourish, protect, and educate their brood knows well enough what I mean.

However, not all birds are so touchingly solicitous toward their young. By human moral standards, the cuckoo, which has no feeling for its eggs and lives in polyandry, must be regarded as irresponsible and shameless. It uses its similarity to the sparrow hawk to frighten sitting songbirds from their nests, and quickly lays an egg in the nest of the involuntary foster mother—which is, incidentally, almost invariably of the same species as the cuckoo's own foster parents. The hungry young cuckoo grows so fast that there is soon no room for the original fledglings, a circumstance which the changeling remedies by simply heaving the young chicks over the edge of the nest! The foster parents do not seem to realize that they have an impostor in their nest and feed it until it is fully fledged, and often for another three weeks after that—no easy task, as a young cuckoo eats four or five times as much as most young birds.

And yet the resonant, somewhat mocking call of the cuckoo in spring tells us that the winter is really over and that nothing can deprive us of the young green of the awakening woods. And—a little superstition can do no harm—lovers with no nest of their own do well to make a wish when the cuckoo calls!

The more acquainted we become with the various species of birds, the more meaningful and appropriate their names appear; names like kingfisher, goldfinch, goatsucker, robin redbreast, yellowhammer, fieldfare, nightingale, tree creeper, and nightjar all demonstrate that man regards his feathered friends as personalities and appreciates them as such.

Descriptions of the various kinds of birdsong have always been popular with poets: the silvery hammering of the chaffinch, for example, and the chattering of the starling, the mournful undertone in the voice of the redbreast, the melodious fluting of the blackbird, and the jubilation of the lark! In likening birdsong to human music they humanize something which is in fact no more than a purely animal sound intended for a specific purpose—i.e., the seeking of a mate of the same species, the marking out of breeding territory, or the result of certain stimuli in the glands of the bird. This understanding, however, should by no means rob us of our very real and justified pleasure in the singing of the birds!

We also tend to accept the coloring of birds as self-evident and forget that nature has given them their feathers as camouflage, as a means of recognizing other birds of the same species, and, above all, for the enticement of the opposite sex; for it is a fact that the bird's spring plumage plays a large part in the propagation and preservation of the species.

In high summer the woods grow silent. The voices of the birds are stilled, mating time is over, and for most birds breeding and rearing time begins. It is nature's period of quietness and contemplation, the season of approaching ripeness. This is the time to go and lie beneath the trees and gaze up to the sky between the branches . . . peace and fulfillment are in everything.

The birds around me hopp'd and play'd,
Their thoughts I cannot measure :—
But the least motion which they made,
It seem'd a thrill of pleasure.

William Wordsworth
from "Lines Written in Early Spring"

IN THE GREAT GREEN STILLNESS

Sometimes, in the calmness of a great wood, a stillness overtakes you beneath the spreading branches of the pines. An unoppressive, soothing stillness which is not silence: soft birdcalls are present, and the humming of unseen insects, the gleam of gossamer in the branches. It is as if the woods were breathing. The light falls in steep, narrow shafts between the trees, gets caught up in the branches, trickles over the white gleaming leaves, and slides across yellow grasses on a warm carpet of dark-green moss and pine needles. The stillness may overtake you on the edge of a glade filled with shimmering heat; or by a stream whose indolent water has ceased to murmur and is sleeping; or on the scalding slopes of a mountain bordered by alder bushes, birches, and silver willows, where ferns quiver gently in the breath of noon.

A wealth of life thrives in the stillness: mosses and fungi, flowers and herbs; ivy creeps crookedly over moss-covered stones and reaches up for tree trunks and stumps; horsetails prosper in profusion, spruce seedlings sprout, beetles and butterflies crawl and flutter—all the early promise of shoots and blossom is fulfilled!

The carpet of wood sorrel laid by the mild spring has grown darker and has threadbare patches. The densely growing wood garlic has lost its white stars, and the scent of the woodruff has long since faded. The poisonous fruit in the lacquered green leaves of the herb Paris is round and swollen, and the delicate "periscopes" on the dark-green cushions of moss watch and wait. In the little-frequented depths of the wood the yellow dead nettle is still in flower, and the wine-red of the purple dead nettle gleams from the undergrowth by the stream. The mysterious violet of a lonely columbine peers out of the cool dimness, and a forgotten lady's-slipper glows against the blackish green.

Strange flowers, barely visible in the dense undergrowth, stand motionless beneath the light, an alien fragrance revealing their iden-

tity: rare orchids, with names as singular as their appearance: tway-blade, soldier orchid, satyrion, or the more approachable early purple orchid. Unlovely and almost shamefaced, the bird's-nest orchid grows in a corner of the wood; it looks sick as it stands there, brown and leafless, living on rotted organic matter. Orchids are indeed a law unto themselves: dependent for their growth and development on the cooperation of fungi, they have at the end of their roots an arrangement which may be described as a kind of working agreement between the plant and the fungi, as it were, a fungi-root nourishment zone which enables the orchid to obtain its nutrition. Naturally, the fungi in question are not the coveted mushrooms, the chanterelles and morels, but tiny organisms which, together with bacteria and other organisms in the soil, extract nourishment from the earth for the orchids.

My modest knowledge of edible fungi forbids me to invite you to accompany me on a mushroom hunt, even though I do know that certain small, air-dried toadstools are just as good as chanterelles in *risotto*. I know a fungi gourmet—and he's still alive to tell the tale—who assures me that finely chopped death-cap toadstools cooked in pastry are a delicacy of the first order; he is also one of those rare epicures who seasons his goulash with orange agaric instead of paprika. Russian Cossack literature is the source of both recipes . . . but this is no place to discuss literature.

Sometimes I believe I can hear the breathing of the woods; but perhaps it is only the influence of the aromas which waft through them: the heavy, narcotic scent of goatsbeard, the acrid aroma of juniper, and the resin of balsam. It was not until I made the acquaintance of the cuckoopint—which at first I took for a tropical plant that had found its way into our woods by mistake—that I found out that some plants do in fact produce a respiratory warmth. The cuckoopint seems almost to exaggerate in this respect, for the fleshy purple spadix at the end of its inflorescence becomes so warm in the "cauldron" of its tall leaves that it literally gives out heat like an oven—for disbelievers I can quote the evidence of experienced naturalists who have measured a temperature of up to forty degrees centigrade. What is the point of this heat? It is the cuckoopint's way of enticing flies into the "cauldron" of its leaves, where they distribute pollen to the female flowers.

Nature is not always as extravagant as this, but it always exhibits what seems to us human beings a boundless profusion. For we cannot conceive of how much pollen it takes to produce a single seedling—of how many seeds must fall to earth, carried by the wind, birds, or animals and deposited at random, for better or for worse. The multitude and multiformity of living things which subsist and reproduce is immeasurable.

Perhaps the beetles and butterflies arouse the greatest wonder. How is it possible for nature to have created so much radiance and beauty, so much variety of form and color? And what is her purpose? Why does the stag beetle carry such an awesome weapon which, by the way, is no more than a greatly enlarged pair of jaws? Is it really for the sole purpose of fighting a dramatic battle with its rival in the mating season? Itself a harmless, peaceable insect which feeds upon the sap of the oak, it would be better served by a different kind of weapon when a hungry jay spots it as a victim.

The oil beetle has a better arrangement: when danger threatens, it exudes from its leg joints an oily brown substance which, although it has no strong aroma, apparently tastes so horrible that the birds disdain the insect as food. Why do bees and wasps have stings, and why do ants live in colonies? Why do some insects have four wings and others only two? Why do some ladybirds have two spots, others seven, ten, sixteen, or eighteen?

Apparently all these creatures are necessary to the over-all plan of creation; they are part of the wonderful and mysterious pattern of life, and we can sense that somehow they all have their value on some higher plane. But, above all, they are beautiful. In jungles of moss, in dusty soil, and in cracks in bark live beetles of the blue of polished steel, the gold of old jewelry, or the green of emeralds—colors and textures reminiscent of jewels, of shining metal; green overlaid with light bronze, brown with a sheen of topaz, black with a hint of silver, fiery golden-red, the yellow of brass, the iridescent brown of quartz. Nature has provided even the smallest and least noticeable of insects with glowing colors, with gaily striped, bizarrely patterned and finely speckled wing cases, with pink, yellow, and blue iridescent wings, with delicately tinted legs and antennae. Many of them are fantastic both in form and behavior; some imitate leaves or escutcheons, some have imposing, frightening antennae or monstrous growths of hair, some act as if they were dead, and some produce evil-smelling substances or even acid, like the ant.

Upon the butterflies nature has bestowed the whole range of pastel colors. On hair-thin wings, the small blues wear the radiance of summer skies; warm as plush is the golden brown of the fritillaries; the gold of pollen adorns the wings of the clouded yellow; and pale, powdery green shimmers on the silken mantle of the green-oak bell moth. And the velvet creatures which fly silently through the fragrant darkness at dusk or in the night, the eyes of owls or peacocks painted on their wings: the emperor moth has a face drawn upon its wings, and the painted eyes stare as deeply and darkly as the night itself.

Nature has not forgotten any of her creatures: the snake and the frog, the snail and the newt—they all have their own peculiar and individual beauty. And although the somber camouflage of the toad may seem rather modest, the common frog sports some reddish spots and back legs striped with brown. The red-brown adder has a fine black zigzag pattern down its back, and the grass snake is richly decked with colored patterns. Even the legless blindworm is sheathed in shimmering bronze, and the emerald lizard is named for his cloak of radiant green.

Anyone who has experienced the great green stillness of the woods possesses a precious gift. Though his hands may be empty—for who would wish to ravage the woodland flowers?—he knows with surety that he has seen nature face to face, has been enchanted by the magic of the woods.

Very old are the woods;
And the buds that break
Out of the brier's boughs,
When March winds wake.

Walter de la Mare
from "All That's Past"

BEFORE DEW AND DAWN

My good relations with my woodsman and hunter friend were based on a tacit agreement never to speak unless it was essential. If something needed explaining—tracks, maybe, or droppings—the discussion usually took place long afterward when we were sitting in a glade in the midday heat, contemplatively chewing our slices of bacon or pale, crumbly cheese. If he had already completed his day's work, he would take his time and, producing an old mess tin dating from his military-service days, he would brew a pale brown coffee seasoned with cloves or cinnamon and laced with a generous dash of schnapps—an infernal drink. Then he would begin to talk. Once he told me about a fox he and his father had coveted for many years after it had stolen half their poultry—always at noon, in full sun—which finally drowned, yes, drowned, in a liquid manure pit. And about the only wildcat he had ever seen, but never shot. Yes, and about the badger... if you were lucky, he said, you could see the female badger in late March evenings as she rustled through the dry foliage and reversed into her burrow while the young badgers played outside.

Occasionally he spoke of "his" red deer—"his" because he had  stalked it year after year. It must have been a magnificent animal, large and very dark, with a chest as broad as a horse's. He never tried to shoot it, at first because he did not have the right kind of gun, and then because he was away on military duty. When he returned, the deer had disappeared, which was not unusual, he said. Sometimes a deer would vanish, unexpectedly overtaken by death, like an old man; or frozen in a winter so cold that the birds dropped lifeless from the branches and the trees split with a crack like an explosion; or shot by someone from the town. He called the deer "the black one" and spoke of it in a voice tinged both with envy and respect. I don't believe he ever really recovered—at any rate not as a hunter—from his disappointment over the animal.

Once a year he would take wife and children in his horse-drawn vehicle to the big autumn market in the nearest town. For this trip he wore a long-sleeved jacket of marten fur, made from the skins of a dozen of the finest pine martens. He wore it proudly and with careless dignity. I do not know what made me ask him if he caught the martens all himself. "No," he answered seriously, "one of them, the last one, chased after me." I was baffled. What did he mean? "The furrier wouldn't wait any longer for the twelfth skin. . . ."

Why do I tell this story? Because I think he was an unusual man and his deeds are worth relating. Actually not so much his deeds as the way he taught us to know and love the woods. I will never forget his words: "Young deer are like children!" Early one morning, long before the sun had sucked the dew from the long grasses, I too was privileged to watch young deer. Through the green of the fresh May undergrowth appeared the head and then the shoulders of a deer which scented the air for a few seconds and then came out into the light and turned to call its young: delicate creatures, staggering awkwardly around their mother and peering into the light with evident surprise. I can still see the eyes of a fawn lying wet and shivering at the foot of a pine tree, gazing fearfully at us with questioning, imploring eyes. . . .

Must we human beings always represent the enemies of animals? But the fawn need not have been afraid; it had been born in one of Europe's many great forest game preserves, from the French Mercantour in the Maritime Alps to Bialowieza in Poland and the Russian Prioksko-Terrasnyi, from the Finnish Unastunturi to the Aosta valley and the Abruzzi mountains. The young deer would grow up in the freedom and security of one of these preserves which, thanks largely to government backing, we have wrested from an ever-expanding population. For what reason? Is it really only because of the feeling that a scarcity of game is an impoverishment of nature? Or do we secretly aspire to pay off an old debt to creation in general—to forgotten, maltreated, devastated life!

In these preserves, reservations, and national parks, red deer, roe, fallow deer, chamois, ibex, wild boar, wolves, bison, and bears live and reproduce; indeed, in some places their rate of increase has already started to give rise to concern. For how can the woods support their increasing numbers, how can we help the animals in winter, and how can we protect them from sickness and from the perils of the roads and railway tracks? No small problem, when we read that in a medium-sized area in a European country with average population and traffic, over nine hundred deer were killed on the roads and railway tracks in just one year—more than a third of the number shot by hunters!

Thus it becomes increasingly clear that the areas in which wild animals can live in peace and safety must be moved farther from civilization and the human beings who seek their company. There are reservations which have been allowed to grow and develop in their natural and original form, untouched and uninfluenced by man; and it is to these areas that we—young people above all—should go from time to time, back to the stillness, to the green wilderness: to rise before dew and dawn, lose ourselves in the woods, and not return before we have encountered the dark gaze of the wild animals.

The play of the hawks and their harsh cry over the treetops . . . the almost ceremonious procession of a family of deer as they leave their daytime abode and fill the glade for a few moments with the golden brown of their bodies before entering the thicket and the peace of night . . . the fearful peeping of the mouse when it senses an owl in the vicinity . . . the barking of a fox in the cool of the night . . . the silent woodland pond, the dark stream, the wild moor. . . . The far-off, secret, ancient woods will show you all this if you will but let them. A foreign country, strange and wonderful.

I believe that the ancient hunting instinct lives on in us all, inhibited though it may be by laws and conventions, ousted from the memory and buried deep in the subconscious. But the old urges awaken when we encounter wild animals, and we too grow wild once more, possessed of a spirit which cannot be denied or thwarted. Thus many a man will be moved to buy a gun and acquire a license and set out to stalk the noble deer, only to find that he cannot kill, will not kill. Our ancestors regarded animals as powerful beings, as superior creatures to be approached with fear and with the last vestiges of strength. And the woods were hostile, trackless wildernesses which harbored savage beasts.

It was the ax which first opened up paths and showed man how to live in the woods when strange, warlike tribes drove him from the restricted regions of the open pastures. A great unrest came over mankind, and the different tribes wandered abroad and became lost in time and space.

The woods became a place of refuge, an abode, and in their untrodden depths the hermit erected his cell, assisted—or so the pious legends tell us—by the bear. The legends are dead now, the woodland chapels abandoned and disintegrated, the unicorn with the fairy tale eyes vanished; and yet the woods remain a place of refuge for homeless, desperate and sensitive human beings, for travelers and, in bitter, needy times of war, for dispersed troops and partisans.

Man's flight from the cities back to nature reveals—if I am not much mistaken—a deeply rooted need for liberation from an oppression which does not lie in outward circumstances alone. Perhaps we sense that we have lost something which we could call peace of mind and spirit, a satisfaction of the heart. A great lassitude comes upon us sometimes, an aversion to senseless activity, an uneasiness and a dissatisfaction with ourselves—or with that part of ourselves which searches for a deeper meaning to our existence, for harmony and a certainty which will give us peace. We could well find it in the woods.

We all know the ancient longing for the tranquillity of the woods, their stillness and their serene magic. And so it could be that you too will leave the narrowness of the confused and fearful, sleeping city and return to the woods for a day of great and true fulfillment. Early, before dew and dawn. . . .

The groves
were God's first temples.

William Cullen Bryant
from "A Forest Hymn"

Acknowledgments All photographs by
WALTER TILGNER
with the exception of
Winter Prather 10/11
Theo Frey 56, 80/81
Ernst Zbären 61, 76
Hans Dossenbach 74
H. W. Silvester 79

Excerpt from "God's Grandeur,"
from *Poems of Gerard Manley
Hopkins,* edited by W. H. Gardner,
Oxford University Press.

"The Red Branch," from
Blue Juniata: Collected Poems by
Malcolm Cowley, Copyright 1947
by Malcolm Cowley.
Originally appeared in *The New
Yorker.*
Reprinted by permission of The
Viking Press, Inc.

Excerpt from "The Example,"
from *The Complete Poems of
W. H. Davies,* Copyright © 1963
by Jonathan Cape Limited.
Reprinted by permission of
Jonathan Cape Limited and
Wesleyan University Press,
publishers.

Excerpt from "All That's Past,"
from *Collected Poems* of Walter de
la Mare, 1941 (Henry Holt and
Company, New York; Faber &
Faber Ltd., London). Reprinted by
permission of The Literary
Trustees of Walter de la Mare and
The Society of Authors, London.

Excerpt from "Sunday Morning,"
Copyright 1923, renewed 1951 by
Wallace Stevens.
Reprinted from *The Collected Poems
of Wallace Stevens* by permission
of Alfred A. Knopf, Inc.

Excerpt from "Green Symphony",
by John Gould Fletcher from
Preludes and Symphonies.
Copyright 1930 by John Gould
Fletcher. Reprinted by permission
of Mrs. John Gould Fletcher.